THE CIVIL WAR

TURNING POINTS OF THE CIVIL WAR

by Russell Roberts

FOCUS READERS.

VOYAGER

www.focusreaders.com

Focus Readers is distributed by North Star Editions:
sales@northstareditions.com | 888-417-0195

Produced for Focus Readers by Red Line Editorial.

Content Consultant: Dr. Gideon Mailer, Associate Professor of History, University of Minnesota Duluth

Photographs ©: U.S. Army Signal Corps/AP Images, cover, 1; Julian Vannerson/Library of Congress, 4–5; akg-images/Newscom, 7; Library of Congress, 8–9, 10, 22–23, 26, 34–35, 40–41; AP Images, 13, 39; Picture History/Newscom, 14–15, 21, 42; Red Line Editorial, 16, 31; Everett Historical/Shutterstock Images, 18, 28–29; George N. Barnard/Library of Congress, 25; Timothy H. O'Sullivan/Library of Congress, 32; Harris & Ewing/Harris & Ewing Collection/Library of Congress, 37; Circa Images/Newscom, 45

Library of Congress Cataloging-in-Publication Data
Names: Roberts, Russell, 1953- author.
Title: Turning points of the Civil War / by Russell Roberts.
Description: Lake Elmo : Focus Readers, 2020. | Series: The Civil War |
    Includes bibliographical references and index. | Audience: Grades 7-9
Identifiers: LCCN 2019031735 (print) | LCCN 2019031736 (ebook) | ISBN
    9781644930854 (hardcover) | ISBN 9781644931646 (paperback) | ISBN
    9781644933220 (pdf) | ISBN 9781644932438 (ebook)
Subjects: LCSH: United States--History--Civil War,
    1861-1865--Campaigns--Juvenile literature. | Gettysburg, Battle of,
    Gettysburg, Pa., 1863--Juvenile literature. | Vicksburg
    (Miss.)--History--Siege, 1863--Juvenile literature.
Classification: LCC E470 .R59 2020 (print) | LCC E470 (ebook) | DDC
    973.7/3--dc23
LC record available at https://lccn.loc.gov/2019031735
LC ebook record available at https://lccn.loc.gov/2019031736

Printed in the United States of America
Mankato, MN
012020

ABOUT THE AUTHOR

Russell Roberts is an award-winning freelance writer who has written and published more than 75 books for both children and adults. His children's books include biographies, examinations of famous buildings, and stories about characters from Greek mythology.

TABLE OF CONTENTS

CHAPTER 1

UNBEATABLE GENERAL LEE

General Robert E. Lee rode his horse into a clearing near Chancellorsville, Virginia. All around him, soldiers cheered. It was May 1863. The US Civil War was in full force. Two years earlier, 11 Southern states had **seceded** to form the Confederate States of America. These states did not want the US government to limit the expansion of slavery. Now, the states were fighting the Union army from the North.

Robert E. Lee was the main commander of the Confederate States Army.

At first, the Union's main goal was making the Southern states rejoin. But by 1863, it began focusing on ending slavery in the South. And black Americans hoped slavery would be made illegal in all states if the Union won the war.

Lee was a Confederate general. He commanded the Army of Northern Virginia. During the Battle of Chancellorsville, his army fought 80,000 Union soldiers commanded by General Joseph Hooker. Lee had only 60,000 men. He was outnumbered. But because of his daring battle strategy, the Confederates won. Lee's troops even set fire to the Union army's headquarters. The large house still burned as the soldiers celebrated.

Lee had defeated the Union army several times before. Recent battles had given the South key strategic victories. In December 1862, for example, the two armies clashed near the town

▲ The Battle of Fredericksburg left several houses in ruins.

of Fredericksburg, Virginia. The Union suffered nearly 13,000 **casualties**. The Confederates had fewer than 5,000.

In the North, all these losses began taking a toll. The war was growing unpopular. Union leaders believed the North needed to win a major battle to help improve **morale**. They hoped it would act as a turning point in the war and lead the Union to victory.

CHAPTER 2

A CONFEDERATE STRONGHOLD

While Hooker struggled against General Lee in the east, another Union army fought the Confederates in the west. This army, called the Army of the Tennessee, was led by General Ulysses S. Grant.

Grant knew the Union desperately needed a strategic victory. So, he made plans to capture the city of Vicksburg, Mississippi. This city stood on bluffs high above the Mississippi River.

Ulysses S. Grant commanded the Army of the Tennessee, the main Union army in the west.

In the early 1860s, approximately 4,500 people lived in Vicksburg, Mississippi.

The Mississippi played a key role in the North's economy. Ships and boats carried farm products from the Midwest down to New Orleans. From the New Orleans port, the products were shipped all over the world.

When Mississippi seceded from the Union, Vicksburg became part of the Confederacy. The city's many guns and cannons shot any Union ships that passed. As long as the Confederates held Vicksburg, Union ships could not use the river. But if Union troops captured Vicksburg, they could reopen this shipping route. They could also keep supplies from reaching much of the South.

Many of the Confederacy's supplies came from Texas, Louisiana, and Arkansas. These supplies included cotton, sugar, rice, horses, cattle, and more. Railroads carried these supplies east to the rest of the Confederacy. If Union soldiers seized Vicksburg, they could stop these shipments. Without supplies, the Confederates would struggle to keep fighting.

Capturing Vicksburg would not be easy. The city was guarded by 172 guns, 8 miles (13 km) of defensive structures, and 30,000 soldiers. Dense woods surrounded much of the city. So did swamps filled with alligators and snakes. It was impossible for an army to move men or heavy equipment over such ground.

The Union had tried to capture Vicksburg before. But every attempt failed. Nevertheless, Grant was determined to try again. He spent hours studying maps and charts, searching for a way to attack the city. He had soldiers dig canals and look for ways to get through the swamps. All these efforts failed. People in the North began demanding that Grant be replaced. They wanted President Abraham Lincoln to choose a new general to lead the Union troops.

In early 1863, however, Grant formed a plan. He would move his army along the Mississippi River to New Carthage, Louisiana. This town was approximately 20 miles (32 km) south of Vicksburg, on the other side of the river. Grant would send ships down the river to meet the army at New Carthage. These ships would carry the soldiers over to Vicksburg.

Confederate guns sank the USS *Cairo* on the Yazoo River near Vicksburg in December 1862.

This plan involved many risks. First, the ships had to get past Vicksburg's guns. Then, the soldiers had to cross the Mississippi. If the Confederates guessed his plan, Grant's small group of soldiers would be easy to defeat. And if they did cross the river, Grant's soldiers would be in enemy territory without supplies. Despite these dangers, Grant prepared to move ahead.

CHAPTER 3

THE ATTACK ON VICKSBURG

On the night of April 16, 1863, Vicksburg held a grand ball. Suddenly, the roar of gunfire interrupted the music and dancing. The Confederates had spotted 11 Union ships sneaking past the city.

Vicksburg's guns blasted the Union ships. They fired more than 500 shots. But only one ship sank. The other 10 made it to New Carthage. Six days later, five more Union ships slipped past.

These Confederate guns sat 200 yards (183 m) from the Mississippi River.

The first part of the plan had been a success. Grant didn't want the Confederates to guess the rest of his plan. So, he had a group of soldiers pretend they were going to attack north of Vicksburg. At the same time, he sent a Union **cavalry** raid through central Mississippi.

Both **diversions** worked. The Confederates focused on these attacks and missed what Grant

➤ THE VICKSBURG CAMPAIGN (1863)

was doing at New Carthage. On April 30, Grant's army crossed the river unopposed. They were now on the Vicksburg side.

General John C. Pemberton led the Confederate forces in Vicksburg. Another Confederate general, Joseph Johnston, urged Pemberton to abandon the city. Johnston wanted to join forces with Pemberton and attack Grant. He thought they could defeat the Union general together and regain control of Vicksburg later on. But Pemberton refused. He had orders from Confederate president Jefferson Davis to defend Vicksburg. And he was determined to stay put.

In mid-May, Pemberton sent soldiers out to defend the roads leading toward the city. On May 16, the two armies met at Champion Hill. Both sides lost hundreds of men. Eventually, the Union troops forced the Confederates to retreat.

▲ The *New York Times* used this illustration in an article about the siege of Vicksburg in 1863.

The armies fought again the next day at the Big Black River. Once again, the Union won. The Confederates fled back inside Vicksburg.

Grant attacked the city on May 19 and May 22. Grant had a much larger army than Pemberton. But Pemberton's men had built trenches and other defenses around the city. Many Union soldiers were killed, and both assaults failed.

So, Grant began a **siege** of Vicksburg instead. Union troops surrounded the city. Nothing could get in or out. Vicksburg was cut off from the rest of the Confederacy. Pemberton's troops had no way to get more supplies. And they didn't have many to begin with. Many people hoped Johnston would come to their rescue. Johnston had gathered 30,000 men. But he didn't think they could break through Grant's troops and stop the siege. The city of Vicksburg was on its own.

Meanwhile, Grant's army was only getting stronger. Soon it numbered 70,000. The giant army bombarded the city with guns and shells. Both sides knew it was only a matter of time before Vicksburg's supplies ran out.

THINK ABOUT IT ◄

Unlike a battle, a siege can last for weeks or even months. What are the advantages of this kind of attack? What are the disadvantages?

LIDA AND WILLIE LORD

The siege of Vicksburg was devastating for the city's civilians. After the war, Lida Lord described what it was like to live there. She wrote that her family was often hungry and thirsty. Soldiers had it even worse. Many "were living on mule meat and bread made of ground beans."[1]

As supplies of food and medicine ran low, people became desperate. Lida wrote that people ate whatever they could find, including "rats and mice and cats and puppies."[2] Wagons rolled through the city every day to collect the dead and bring them to the cemetery.

In addition, Union **artillery** constantly pounded the city with shells. To avoid being hurt or killed, many people left their homes. They moved to caves dug into the city's hills. But even there,

▲ Camps built by soldiers covered the hills near Vicksburg.

they were not safe. People risked being bitten by mosquitoes and snakes.

Plus, shells could still reach the caves, causing some to collapse. One shell hit the hill where Lida's family was hiding. Her brother Willie described how the shell "detached a great mass of crumbling earth from one side of the roof." This falling earth "crushed a young woman to the floor of a cave."[3] The woman survived. But many civilians died in similar collapses.

1. A. A. Hoehling. *Vicksburg: 47 Days of Siege*. Mechanicsburg, PA: Stackpole Books, 1969. 205.
2. Hoehling. *Vicksburg*. 201.
3. Hoehling. *Vicksburg*. 215.

CHAPTER 4

INVADING THE NORTH

As the Union army bore down on Vicksburg in May 1863, Jefferson Davis called General Lee to Richmond for a strategy conference. Davis wanted to save Vicksburg. He wanted to send some of Lee's troops to Mississippi to fight Grant.

Lee disagreed. He didn't think the siege could last through the summer. Summers in Mississippi could be very hot and humid. Lee believed this weather would force the Union troops to retreat.

Jefferson Davis lived in this house in Richmond, Virginia, from August 1861 to April 1865.

Instead, Lee wanted to move his army north and invade Pennsylvania.

At the conference, Lee explained his thinking. He listed several benefits of the invasion. Much of the fighting so far had occurred in Virginia. The state's farms had been stripped bare of food and livestock to feed the army. And battles had destroyed large areas of land, including several towns.

By invading the North, Lee could draw both armies out of Virginia. Confederate troops could attack cities in the North. They could also find food in Pennsylvania's rich farm country.

To defend this territory, the Union forces would have to move north as well. This would give Virginia a chance to recover. Union troops might even leave Vicksburg to help stop the invasion. In fact, people in the North might pressure President

△ Several key battles, such as the Battle of Seven Pines, took place in Virginia.

Lincoln to focus on defending their land from attack.

An invasion would also show that the South was determined to keep fighting. Lee hoped that European countries might offer **diplomatic recognition** to the Confederacy. This important offer could help establish the Confederacy as a separate nation. So far, the Union refused to view the Confederacy as a real country. But if a country such as France or the United Kingdom recognized the Confederacy, Lee hoped the Union might, too.

George Gordon Meade (center) poses with his staff.

Even if this didn't happen, winning a battle on Northern ground would fuel the growing movement of people in the North who wanted the war to end.

Davis approved Lee's idea. So, on June 3, 1863, Lee's army began heading north from Virginia. The group of approximately 70,000 soldiers marched through Maryland and into Pennsylvania. They were amazed at the green landscapes and prosperous farms. Soldiers walked right up to farmhouses and asked for food. Often they received it. A Southern general wondered if they would all get too fat.

Hooker's Army of the Potomac followed the Confederates out of Virginia. Hooker's soldiers stayed between the Confederate army and Washington, DC. That way, Lee could not suddenly attack the Union capital.

However, after the defeats at Chancellorsville and Fredericksburg, Hooker was losing support as a leader. He resigned on June 28. General George Gordon Meade replaced him. Meade was the army's fifth commander in the last 10 months.

THINK ABOUT IT ◁

The Army of the Potomac changed commanders several times. What advantages could come from a new leader? Can you think of any disadvantages?

CHAPTER 5

THE BATTLE OF GETTYSBURG BEGINS

By late June, Lee's army had spread out across several miles of southern Pennsylvania. On June 28, a Confederate spy reported that the Army of the Potomac was in Frederick, Maryland. The Confederates had thought the Union soldiers were still in Virginia. Lee ordered his scattered army to reunite. He wanted to be ready if Meade attacked. On the morning of July 1, a large group of Confederate soldiers moved toward Gettysburg.

Roads and high ground near Gettysburg, Pennsylvania, made the town a strategic location.

This town was near the place where Lee's army would gather. Unknown to them, Union soldiers lay in wait behind fences and trees.

The Union soldiers had entered Gettysburg the day before. Unlike Lee, who often lacked information about the location of Union troops, Meade was well informed about the Confederates' movements. He knew Lee's soldiers were nearby, and he expected them to head toward Gettysburg. Roads led into the town from many directions. And several areas of high ground surrounded it. The high ground would be easy to defend. Union soldiers occupied these areas to watch for an attack.

As the Confederate soldiers approached the town, the Union soldiers spotted them. At 7:30 a.m., a Union soldier fired a shot. The Confederates returned fire. The battle had begun.

Drawn by the sound of gunfire, reinforcements for both sides raced to Gettysburg. Soon the town was in chaos. By late afternoon, the Union army had retreated to the high ground outside of town. Many soldiers gathered on Cemetery Hill.

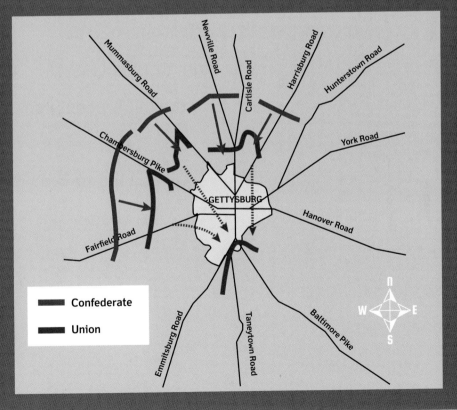

GETTYSBURG (JULY I, 1863)

Union troops built fortifications on a hill called Little Round Top.

To win the battle, the Confederates needed to drive the Union off this high ground. Lee told General Richard Ewell to take the hill if possible. But Ewell did not try.

All night long, the Union soldiers built defenses on the high ground. By morning, they had built a defensive line shaped like a fishhook. This line stretched 3 miles (4.8 km) among the hills, trees, and ridges.

General James Longstreet urged Lee to swing the Confederate army around the Union's left

flank. That would put the Confederates between the Union army and Washington, DC. Union troops would have to leave Gettysburg and follow the Confederates, or they would risk losing their capital. However, Lee had a different plan in mind. He wanted to attack the Union army. Longstreet reluctantly agreed and got ready to fight.

On July 2, Confederate and Union soldiers fought all day on the fields and hills around Gettysburg. Each army lost nearly 9,000 men. But when night came, the two armies were about where they had been in the morning. The Battle of Gettysburg was not over yet.

THINK ABOUT IT ◄

Why would higher ground be easier for soldiers to defend than lower ground?

CHAPTER 6

PICKETT'S CHARGE

On the afternoon of July 3, 150 Confederate artillery began firing at the Union troops on Cemetery Ridge. However, most aimed too high. Their shells sailed over the Union soldiers' heads. Approximately 75 Union guns responded.

The guns quieted around 3:00 p.m. More than 10,000 Confederate soldiers lined up. The men were led by General George Pickett. They planned to cross an open field toward the Union forces.

Like many Confederate generals, George Pickett had previously served in the US Army.

General Longstreet opposed this plan. Approximately 6,000 Union soldiers defended Cemetery Ridge. The Confederate troops would have to travel nearly a mile uphill with Union troops firing down on them. Longstreet feared the charge would fail. Worse, he thought many soldiers would be killed. But Lee ordered the attack to go ahead anyway.

As Pickett's men ran across the field, bullets rained down on them. The Confederate soldiers had no place to take cover. Thousands were killed. Only a few hundred men broke through the Union defenses. But those men were quickly driven back.

The disastrous attack became known as Pickett's Charge. The Confederates lost more than 6,000 men. A few soldiers struggled back across the field. Lee met these survivors. He sadly admitted that this disaster had been all his fault.

Marines reenact Pickett's Charge in 1922.

The Confederates expected a counterattack. But none came. General Meade had been in command for only six days. Three of these days had been spent fighting at Gettysburg. Meade was happy just to have stopped the Confederate attack.

Pickett's Charge was Lee's last attempt at victory. On July 4, in driving rain, he began retreating back to Virginia. The invasion of the North was over.

VOLUNTEER NURSES

Both sides suffered devastating losses at Gettysburg. When the two armies marched south, they left more than 20,000 wounded soldiers behind. Only a small group of doctors and nurses were left to care for them.

Homes and churches near the battlefield were used as hospitals. Mary McAllister, a volunteer nurse, described the scene in one church. "Every pew was full," she wrote. Some soldiers were "sitting, some lying, some leaning on others." Volunteers worked "wetting cloths and putting them on the wounds."[1]

Many soldiers had been hurt so badly they needed to have limbs amputated. McAllister wrote that the overwhelmed surgeons "cut off the legs and arms and threw them out of the windows."[2] Sometimes bandages ran out. Volunteers tore off pieces of their own clothing to use as bandages.

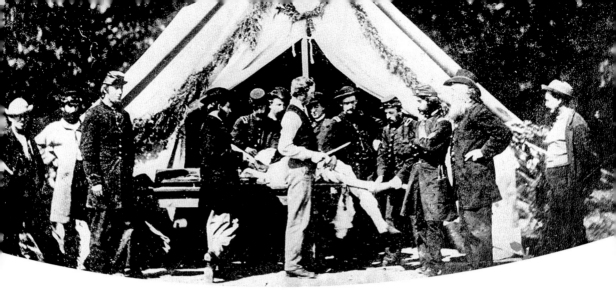

▲ A doctor prepares for an amputation in a tent being used for medical care.

More than 3,000 soldiers from each side had died during the three days of fighting. Their bodies lay on the ground in the hot July sun. Soon they began to smell. Nurse Cornelia Hancock wrote, "A sickening, overpowering, awful stench announced the presence of the unburied dead."[3] Hancock wrote that this smell was even worse than seeing the bodies themselves.

1. Stephen W. Sears. *Gettysburg*. Boston: Houghton Mifflin, 2003. 508.
2. Sears. *Gettysburg*. 508.
3. Cornelia Hancock. *Letters of a Civil War Nurse*. Edited by Henrietta Stratton Jaquette. Lincoln, NE: University of Nebraska Press, 1998. 4–5.

CHAPTER 7

THE TIDE TURNS

The same day Pickett's Charge failed, Pemberton and Grant met outside Vicksburg. As the summer progressed, conditions inside the city had gotten worse. By June, Confederate soldiers received only a handful of food to eat each day. They urged Pemberton to feed them or surrender. By July 3, Pemberton knew he could not continue. He sent men carrying a white flag to Grant, asking to discuss terms for surrender.

Confederate general John C. Pemberton tried to defend the city of Vicksburg as long as possible.

▲ Lincoln (4th from left) worked with several generals, but he had great respect for Grant (6th from left).

The next day, Pemberton agreed to all of Grant's terms. After 47 days, the siege was finally over. Grant's troops marched into Vicksburg. They captured the remaining Confederate soldiers. The important city was back under Union control.

Because of the siege's success, Grant became Lincoln's most trusted general. The two men worked closely together for the rest of the war.

Lincoln believed the Union finally had a general who could oppose Lee.

Both Gettysburg and Vicksburg gave the Union a much-needed boost in morale. These battles were the turning points that the Union needed. On July 4, many Northerners celebrated. Cannons fired 100-gun salutes. Church bells tolled.

There was little joy in the Confederacy. Many people were shocked when they heard the news from Vicksburg. The city's surrender destroyed the South's morale. It also split the Confederacy in half. The Mississippi River now divided its eastern and western sections. A few days later, on July 9, the only remaining Confederate **outpost** on the Mississippi surrendered. The river was once again open to the Midwest.

Lee's invasion had failed. Soon, both the Union and Confederate armies were back in the South.

The Confederates had suffered a devastating 28,000 casualties. That was more than one-third of Lee's army. He would never again have the power to launch an offensive campaign.

Such a huge defeat ended Davis's hopes of diplomatic recognition from Europe. It also dashed his attempts to negotiate peace with Lincoln. Davis had sent his vice president, Alexander Stephens, to Washington, DC. Davis hoped Stephens would arrive as Lee's army was advancing on the city. Faced with an invading army, Lincoln might agree to end the war. Instead, Lincoln refused to even meet with Stephens.

Meanwhile, support for the Union war effort continued to grow. In early 1863, the Emancipation Proclamation had declared all enslaved people in Confederate states free. It also allowed the Union army to recruit black soldiers.

▲ The Emancipation Proclamation allowed black men to serve in the Union army.

Huge numbers of enslaved people escaped to Union camps. Many of them joined the army. Thousands of free black men also enlisted. But because of discrimination, black soldiers fought in few major battles.

The Civil War would continue for nearly two more years. But historians agree that the war turned in the Union's favor at Gettysburg and Vicksburg. And it would not turn back.

FOCUS ON
TURNING POINTS OF THE CIVIL WAR

Write your answers on a separate piece of paper.

1. Write a paragraph summarizing General Robert E. Lee's reasons for invading the North in 1863.

2. Do you think Gettysburg or Vicksburg had a bigger impact on the war's outcome? Why?

3. Which general planned the siege of Vicksburg?

   A. Joseph Hooker
   B. George Gordon Meade
   C. Ulysses S. Grant

4. How would a military victory boost morale in the North?

   A. People would feel more certain that their side could win the war.
   B. People would learn which general was leading the army.
   C. People would stop reading about the fighting in newspapers.

Answer key on page 48.

GLOSSARY

artillery
Large mounted guns or cannons.

casualties
People who are killed, wounded, or missing in battle.

cavalry
A military force with troops who serve on horseback.

diplomatic recognition
When one country formally agrees that the government of another country is real or valid.

diversions
Actions performed to draw an enemy's attention away from another main event.

flank
The right or left side of a military line.

morale
The mood of a group of people, especially people in a difficult situation.

outpost
A fort or camp used by a military to guard against attack, especially when located far from the main army.

seceded
Formally withdrew from a political group or nation.

siege
An attack in which soldiers surround a town or other area and cut off all its supplies in an attempt to force it to surrender.

TO LEARN MORE

BOOKS

Coddington, Andrew. *Code Breakers and Spies of the Civil War*. New York: Cavendish Square, 2018.

Cordell, M. R. *Courageous Women of the Civil War: Soldiers, Spies, Medics, and More*. Chicago: Chicago Review Press, 2016.

Cummings, Judy Dodge. *The Civil War: The Struggle that Divided America*. White River Junction, VT: Nomad Press, 2017.

NOTE TO EDUCATORS

Visit **www.focusreaders.com** to find lesson plans, activities, links, and other resources related to this title.

INDEX

Answer Key: 1. Answers will vary; **2.** Answers will vary; **3.** C; **4.** A